# THE STRATEGIC TAXPAYER
## MANIFESTO

Kim M. Larsen, EA CTFS

This publication is designed to provide competent and reliable information regarding the subject matter covered. However, it is sold with the understanding that the author and publisher are not engaged in rendering legal, financial, or other professional advice. Law and practices often vary from state to state and country to country and if legal or other expert assistance is required, the services of a professional should be sought. The author and publisher specifically disclaim any liability that is incurred from the use or application of the contents of this book.

Copyright © 2022 Kim McKay Larsen

All rights reserved. Except as permitted under the U.S. Copyright Act of 1976, no part of this publication may be reproduced, distributed, or transmitted in any form or by any means or stored in a database or retrieval system, without the prior written permission of the publisher.

Published By

InstraMedia Ltd
www.instramedia.com

ISBN-13: 978-1-959015-01-7

This book is dedicated to my parents
Udell & Laurel Larsen

Prerelease Copy For Your Review

If you like this book and would like to submit a review you can do so on the website for the book at:
www.strategictaxpayer.com
Just click "Submit Your Review" and complete the short review form.
Thanks so much for your interest. Selected reviews will be published in the release version of this book.

# Preface

## *Why Another Book About Taxes?*

I confess, I am a book junkie. I can go on Amazon looking for one title and easily end up buying ten. I have about twenty feet of floor to ceiling bookshelves in my home office, but there is no room for more books now so I have got some books on the floor as well. I buy mostly business books, but being tax strategist, I am keenly interested in any book about reducing taxes, so I think I have at least 50 books on the subject. I have read them all, some were very good and some were not so good. Most of my tax books are around 300-400 pages, but I have one that is almost 900. It's a good thing I am a fast reader. But frankly, most tax books are painful to read because of all the unnecessary details that are included to support readers that won't be getting professional help with their tax issues.

I have written this book as a quick start guide to tax strategy. It is intended to help you understand many important concepts and tools that can be deployed to substantially reduce your taxes. This stuff is complicated, you WILL need the help of an excellent tax advisor to implement many of the strategies I have written about in this book. That being said, all the strategies in this book are what I use on a daily basis in my practice, there is nothing here that is beyond the reach of the typical small business owner. Obviously, the more you make, the more you can save, but you don't need to be listed on the Forbes 400 to benefit from the strategies you will discover here.

I wrote the outline for this book in May of 2020. I was stuck in my home on Maui, waiting out the pandemic so I thought I would write this book. However, our firm got so busy dealing with PPP loans, EIDL and other pandemic related assistance for our clients I never got to write a single word until August of 2022.

I promise, this book will be an easy and fast paced read that will give you just what you need to know to effectively work with your tax advisor to craft the most appropriate tax strategy for your personal and business situations. I can't promise you will save millions, but I bet some readers will!

Kim Larsen<br>
Maui, Hawaii<br>
September 6, 2022

# CONTENTS

Chapter One ............................................................... 1
    Introduction ............................................................. 1
    Taxpayer Types ........................................................ 3
    Two Tax Systems ..................................................... 4
    Lifestyle, Wealth & Taxes ........................................ 6
    Sources of Tax Law ................................................. 9

Chapter Two .............................................................. 12
    Exclude Income ...................................................... 12
        14 Day Augusta ................................................. 12
        Gain on Sale of Personal Residence .................. 14
        Loan Proceeds .................................................. 14
        Life Insurance ................................................... 15
        Qualified Small Business Stock ........................ 16
        Roth IRA Distributions ...................................... 18
        Damages Received For Personal Injury ............ 18
        Gifts Received ................................................... 19
        Municipal Bond Interest ................................... 19

Chapter Three ........................................................... 20
    Shift Income ............................................................ 20
        Kids On Payroll ................................................. 22
        Sale/Lease Back of Equipment ........................ 23
        Gift/Sale of Appreciated Property ..................... 24
        Pay Your C Corporation .................................... 25

Chapter Four ............................................................. 27
    Convert Income ...................................................... 27

    Earned Income to S Corp Distribution … 30

    Ordinary Income to Passive … 31

    Ordinary Income to Capital Gain … 32

Chapter Five … 33

    Defer Income … 33

        Qualified Retirement Plans … 33

        Real Estate Exchange … 35

Chapter Six … 38

    Tax Deduction Strategies … 38

    Depreciation & Amortization … 44

    Deduct Personal Expenses … 45

        Accountable Plans … 46

        Business Travel & Meals … 47

        Medical Expense Reimbursement … 49

        Home Office Reimbursement … 51

        Business Auto Expense … 54

        Exercise Facility … 55

    Tax Incentivized Activities … 55

        Real Estate Investment … 56

            Active Participant … 57

            Qualified Real Estate Professional … 58

            Cost Segregation … 58

        Oil & Gas Investment … 60

        Create Intellectual Property … 61

        Opportunity Zone … 62

    Charitable Deduction Strategies … 62

  Donate Appreciated Property ... 63
  Charitable Remainder Trust ... 64
  Charitable Lead Trust ... 64
  Donor Advised Fund ... 65
  Private Foundations ... 65
  Conservation Easements ... 66
 Qualified Business Income ... 67

Chapter Seven ... 68
 Tax Credits ... 68

Chapter Eight ... 71
 Entities Explained ... 71
 Individual ... 72
 Sole Proprietorship ... 72
 Trust ... 73
 Partnership ... 74
 Corporation ... 76
  C Corporation ... 76
  S Corporation ... 77
 Limited Liability Company ... 78
 Choice of Entity ... 78

Chapter Nine ... 80
 Tax Advisors ... 80
 CPA ... 83
 Enrolled Agent ... 83
 Attorney ... 84
 Knowledge, Experience & Mindset ... 84

    Working With a Tax Strategist ............................................................. 86
Chapter Ten ............................................................................................... 87
    Importance of Record Keeping ........................................................... 87
    A Final Word of Caution ..................................................................... 91

# CHAPTER ONE

## Introduction

### *Are You Overpaying Your Taxes?*

Even the IRS reluctantly admits that year after year millions of taxpayers fail to claim allowable deductions and credits that end up costing millions in overpaid taxes. You may not know it, but you are probably one of them, especially if you are a business owner or investor. The Internal Revenue Code is chocked-full of juicy deductions that only business owners or investors can take advantage of. It almost seems unfair to all the other taxpayers who don't qualify. Obviously, our lawmakers have their reasons for being so generous. But such generosity has its limits. Frankly, no one at the IRS is going to care if you miss a deduction that costs you thousands of dollars in overpaid taxes. On the other hand, if someone at the IRS finds you have taken a deduction you are not entitled to, you can expect them to care a lot.

While the Internal Revenue Code is literally a road map to reduce your taxes, it is indeed a very complicated "road map" that is about 8000 pages of fine print. If you add IRS regulations, Court decisions and other relevant documents you've got another 20000+ pages to consider, and that's a sure cure for insomnia.

Obviously, you want to avoid overpaying your taxes and no doubt, you think an IRS audit would be about as much fun as that root canal you have been putting off. The bottom line here is: you need to know a lot about your taxes in order to avoid overpaying them.

You may be thinking that you don't need to know anything about taxes, because you have a great accountant that "takes care" of all your tax needs! Well, I hate to disappoint you, but that erroneous assumption is responsible for the waste of millions of dollars in overpaid taxes every year.

Let me explain it this way: Even though you have a dentist that "takes care" of your teeth, you certainly understand that you have to do your part (brushing/flossing, etc) on a daily basis otherwise even the best of care by your dentist is not going to prevent major problems. The same is true of your tax situation. While you may only see your accountant once or twice a year, you are doing things everyday that will affect your taxes for better or worse. If you don't know how to properly handle all of these daily issues, you are going to overpay your taxes. Moreover, let's face it, your accountant is busy with a lot of things, besides your taxes. At best, your accountant is a "Monday morning quarterback."

A big part of what I do as a tax strategist is educate my clients about taxes and tax strategy. My primary goal in writing this book is to make the tools and strategies that have been so effective for my clients available to more taxpayers than I can serve on an individual basis.

If you read and apply what you learn from this book, you won't be overpaying your taxes. However, this book is NOT a substitute for a professional tax advisor, so don't even think about doing-it-yourself. Having a tax strategist on your team is an investment, NOT an expense. I will discuss advisors in detail in Chapter nine.

## *What Type of Taxpayer Are You?*

In over forty years of tax practice I have come to understand that there are two types of taxpayers. First, there is the *typical taxpayer* who only thinks about taxes as he is trying to assemble all his tax documents to prepare for his tax preparation appointment. I am sorry to say this is almost everybody.

Then, we have the *strategic taxpayer*™ who understands that just about every financial decision he makes will affect his tax situation for better or worse. This taxpayer wants to proactively manage his taxes so he pays only what he owes and not a penny more. This takes a little time and effort, but, as you will see, the results are more than worth it in the end. Most very wealthy people are *strategic taxpayers.*™

As you can imagine, in my work, I get to answer a lot of tax questions. Most of the time, the answer starts with "It depends." Yes, that's right "It depends on the facts and circumstances."

The *strategic taxpayer*™ knows that by proactively managing his facts and circumstances he can pay the least amount of tax possible under the law.

How do you become a *strategic taxpayer*™? Reading this book will be a great start. Then you need to get with your tax advisor to design a tax and wealth strategy for your unique situation.

## *Two Tax Systems?*

Strange as it sounds, in the United States we actually have two tax systems. The first applies to people who are employed wage earners. The second system applies to business owners and investors. Let's explore how each system works:

## *The Wage Earner System*

With this system the taxpayer's income is reported to the IRS by the employer who also withholds the required income taxes. So the taxpayer never even has access to his total gross income. At the end of the year, the employer gives the taxpayer a W2 form to be filed with his tax return. With this system, the taxpayer is only allowed some very limited deductions from gross income to determine the final tax owed. The taxpayer completes and files an income tax return which reconciles his income, withholding, allowable deductions and credits to determine a refund or balance due amount.

## *The Business Owner/Investor System*

With this system the taxpayer collects his total business income and then gets to deduct all necessary business expenses. Which, as you will see, can include a business allocation of many otherwise personal expenses. Here, the taxpayer is on "the honor system" to determine his net business or investment income and then file a tax return to report the results and pay any taxes due. Yes, the IRS can audit the taxpayer, but if he is following the rules, that's nothing to worry about.

| Wage-Earner System | Bus/Inv System |
|---|---|
| Income | Income |
| - Taxes | - Expenses |
| - Expenses | - Taxes |
| = Cash Flow | = Cash Flow |

## Which System Is Best for You?

The good news is you can actually use both systems, like most of my clients. Even if you have a wonderful job that pays you an outstanding salary, I strongly recommend you consider starting some sort of side-business. You should also be an investor. My investment of choice is real estate, but maybe you will like something else better. Just understand, most of the tax strategies in this book are intended for business owners and investors.

## Three Numbers Everybody Should Know

Most people don't look at it this way, but just about everybody uses their personal income in three basic ways:

### Lifestyle Expenses

These are all the expenses related to maintaining your lifestyle. This would include housing, food, dining out, entertainment, non-business travel, transportation, health care, and personal care.

### *Savings & Investment*

This is money put into savings or other investments that would include contributing to savings accounts, brokerage accounts, IRA/pension accounts, investment real estate and pretty much any other type of investment made during the year.

### *Taxes*

Regardless of how they are paid, everyone making a reasonable living pays taxes on their income. For wage earners, taxes are usually deducted at the source. Business owners and investors, usually pay estimated taxes throughout the year. Both kinds of taxpayers may owe additional taxes or get a refund of any overpayment when their tax returns are filed each year.

So be honest with yourself! Do you know how much of your income went to each of these categories last year? Do you see how managing these numbers could have a substantial impact on your wealth and quality of life in the future?

### *How to Get Started*

The best way is by tracking all of your personal income and expenses with accounting software or an app. This will allow you put each transaction in the appropriate category, so you can really see how your money is being used. Once you have this knowledge you will be better equipped to make choices about your money. Another side benefit of this process is, we almost always find expenses that we can make tax deductible that were being missed. When I do a wealth strategy engagement for a client, this is where we start.

If you can't do the tracking as I suggested above, you can certainly use this simple method which will be better than nothing. With the simple method you use numbers from your tax return and account statements to estimate your numbers. Here's how it works:

a. Find your total income from your tax returns
b. Find your total tax liability from your tax returns
c. Review your savings and investment statements and add up all the investments you have made during the year.
d. On a worksheet or in Excel subtract (b) & (c) from (a). The result will be your estimated lifestyle expenses.
e. Now divide your lifestyle expense by your total income (a)
f. Now divide your tax liability by your total income(a)
g. Now divide your saving & investments (made during the year) by your total income(a)

Your worksheet could look something like this if your total income was $500,000

* * *

| Category | Amount | Percent of Total Inc |
|---|---|---|
| Lifestyle | $250000 | 50% |
| Saving & Investment | $100000 | 20% |
| Taxes | $150000 | 30% |

Keep in mind, this simple method does not take into account any debt you may have incurred during the year, so you may need to adjust accordingly.

### *How to Use These Numbers to Build Your Wealth*

Do these numbers surprise you? Now that you have established some key metrics, you can determine what steps you can take to improve and optimize your results. You can use the strategies in this book to reduce your tax liability and I suggest you use the savings to increase what you can devote to investments.

Obviously, we could go a lot deeper here, but this is a book about tax strategy, not wealth strategy.

Kim Larsen

## *How Is Tax Law Made?*

\* \* \*

There is an old saying "If you like sausage, you don't want to know how it's made." I think that just might be true. And you could probably say the same thing about tax laws. I promise, I am not going to bore you with a lot of unnecessary details, but I will give you a brief overview starting with the "Big Why"

When it comes to getting citizens to act in ways it deems appropriate or not do things it deems inappropriate, a government has three main options:

- Jail or other forms of punishment
- A cash payment or other compensation
- A tax incentive

Obviously, in order to operate, a government needs a source of revenue. Hence, taxes have existed throughout recorded history. Income taxes existed in the United States for brief periods during the late 1800s, but many people believed they were unconstitutional. But in 1913 the Sixteenth Amendment was ratified and it states:

> The Congress shall have the power lay and collect taxes on incomes, from whatever source derived, without apportionment among the several States, and without regard to any census or enumeration.

Since 1913 Congress has used this power to tax for two primary purposes: 1)to bring in revenues and 2)to provide tax incentives to taxpayers that do things that Congress believes will be of greater benefit to our society than the taxes that would otherwise be due.

The tax laws of the United States are found in the Internal Revenue Code, as well as regulations, numerous court decisions and revenue rulings, etc. Most people, including many tax professionals, think the Code is mostly about raising revenue. The reality is that less than 1 percent of the Code is there to raise revenue. The other 99 percent of the Code is a roadmap to reducing taxes by doing the things Congress wants you to do. Your tax advisor needs to be an expert on all of these, but you don't. The pages of this book will give you all you need to know to work with a competent tax advisor and pay the lowest tax possible under the law.

In the following chapters I will go over various types of tax strategies and give you an overview of how you can use them to reduce your taxes. Obviously, not everything I write about will apply to you. That's where you need to work with your tax advisor to determine what's appropriate for your situation.

## CHAPTER TWO

## Exclude Income

In this chapter I will cover all the types of excludable income that I see on a regular basis. Some would say the first rule of income tax is "all income is taxable unless the Code says it isn't." That statement is absolutely true. So when the Internal Revenue Code specifically states that a particular type of income is not taxable, we say it is excludable from income. Please note, this is not a complete list of all types of excludable income If you have any doubt about whether some income you have received is taxable, please consult your tax advisor.

### *14 Day Augusta*

Once upon a time, there was a US Senator that lived in

Augusta, Georgia. This Senator thought it would be great if he could rent out his home during the Masters golf tournament. So much the better if all the rent he collected was not taxable. Well, you guessed it, Congress passed a law allowing homeowners to rent out their homes for up to fourteen days per year and completely exclude any rent received.

*How You Can Take Advantage of the Augusta Rule*

One of my clients was able to rent his home for use as a movie set for two weeks. Most of the time my clients use this to rent their homes to their business for use in offsite meetings or other events, like a holiday party etc. If you want to do this you need to determine a fair rent amount. I suggest you get written quotes from event venues in your area and set your rent accordingly. Obviously, you probably won't hold fourteen days of meetings or events in a row, but you can do this multiple times during the year; just don't exceed fourteen days total.

What makes this deal great is that your business gets a tax deduction for the rent it pays you, but you won't need to pay taxes on the rent you receive.

## *Gain on Sale of Personal Residence*

There are a number of tax advantages to home ownership but one of the best is the opportunity to exclude up to $500,000 of gain when you sell it. In order to qualify for this, you need to have lived in the home as your primary residence for at least two out of the last five years. If you lived in it less than two years you may be able to get a prorated exclusion of something less than the full $500,000. It should be noted that the $500,000 exclusion is available to married taxpayers filing jointly. Other taxpayers get an exclusion of up to $250,000.

What's really terrific about this provision is that there is NO limit on the number of times you can use it! The only limitation is you can only do it once every two years. Imagine buying a fixer-upper every two years and being able to exclude all your profits on the resale.

## *Loan Proceeds*

Because you are obligated to repay a loan, it would seem obvious that loan proceeds would not be taxable. Over the years, I have worked with many clients to use this provision in creative ways that have resulted in substantial tax savings. Let me walk you through two examples:

My client Dave got a great deal on a fixer-upper home. He did all the work and was ready to put the home on the market, but instead he did a refi and got all of his investment back plus about $10,000 of his profit. He still had about 25 percent equity in the home so he got the seller of another property he was buying to carry a second mortgage against the remaining equity. So basically, Dave has all of his investment back and all of his profit without paying any taxes.

My client Larry sold his company to a firm that was acquiring similar companies to do an IPO. The deal was structured as an exchange of stock which is not taxable. Larry was expecting to make a huge profit once the company completed the IPO, but he wanted some cash he could use now. We were able to get the acquiring firm to make Larry a $1 million loan secured by some of the stock he exchanged for. So Larry has $1 million to use but no taxes to pay.

## *Life Insurance*

The death benefit received from a life insurance policy is not taxable, however most payouts include a small amount of interest from the date of the decedent's death that will be taxable. This applies to both term and whole life policies.

One of the benefits of whole life policies is that they accumulate cash value. Depending on the premiums paid and how the policy is structured substantial cash values can be accumulated over time. This cash value can be borrowed against at a very low interest rate. Because accumulations within the policy are not subject to tax the invested funds can grow faster than if they were outside the policy. There are a lot of creative opportunities available depending on your situation. I have a number of clients that are using these policies as a major part of their retirement strategy. The one thing you need to watch out for if you are thinking of doing a whole life policy is how large is the sales load is. With all whole life policies you need to be aware of any surrender charges as well as any other fees. Shop around and make sure you are getting the best deal possible.

## Qualified Small Business Stock

Because one of my offices is located near the Silicon Valley I have been able to work with a number of very successful tech founders. Several of my clients have been able to take advantage of IRC Sec 1202 which allows a taxpayer to exclude 100 percent of gain on the sale of stock up to the greater of $10 million or

10x the basis in the stock. Imagine, selling your company for a $10 million profit and owing no tax! Yes, that's a great deal, but naturally, not everyone qualifies. So let's look at what is required:

- Company must be taxed as a C corporation
- Stock must be acquired directly from the corporation at original issue
- The corporation's gross assets can't be $50 million or more when stock is issued
- Must hold the stock for at least five years before sale

There are some corporations that don't qualify based on what business they are in:

- Personal services
- Financial services
- Farming
- Oil/gas
- Hotel, motel or restaurant

## Roth IRA Distributions

A Roth IRA is an Individual Retirement Account that accepts only after-tax contributions. While you don't get any tax deduction for contributions, all your contributions and earnings grow tax-free. You can withdraw from your account tax and penalty-free after you are 59 1/2 as long as the account has been open at least five years. There are income limitations so not all taxpayers can contribute to a Roth. However, it may still be possible to get funds into a Roth by doing what's called a "back door" contribution, which is essentially doing a rollover from a traditional IRA to a Roth IRA. Doing such a rollover requires you to pay any tax on the funds you rollover.

Having a Roth IRA offers some interesting opportunities if you can invest it well. Imagine if you had bought 1000 shares of Amazon in your Roth IRA back in 2012 when it was trading at around $11 per share. All withdrawals from your Roth would be excluded from income so then are tax-free.

## Damages Received for Personal Injury

Any payments you receive on account of a personal injury are excludable from income under IRC Sec 104(a)(2) However, it should be noted that punitive damages or damages from emotional distress are generally taxable.

The tax strategy when negotiating a personal injury claim would be to allocate as much as possible to physical injuries. A tax advisor should be consulted to help evaluate any potential offers.

## *Gifts Received*

When a taxpayer receives a gift from a relative or friend the amount of such gift is excludable from income and is not taxable. It is possible that the giver of the gift may be required to file a gift tax return, but because of the annual exemption and lifetime exclusion it's unlikely any gift tax would be due.

## *Municipal Bond Interest*

Interest received on municipal bonds is generally tax-free. You can also get the same benefit by investing in a mutual fund that holds qualified municipal bonds. It should be noted, that because bonds are sometimes bought and sold at a discount or premium it is possible to incur a capital gain or loss which would not be tax-exempt.

## CHAPTER THREE

## Shift Income

There are seven federal income tax brackets starting at ten percent and going all the way up to 37 percent. Tax is calculated on a graduated basis as shown in the following tax table which applies to married taxpayers filing joint.

| Tax Rate | Tax Income Bracket | Taxes Owed |
|---|---|---|
| 10% | $0 to $20,550 | 10 % of taxable income |
| 12% | $20,551 to $83,550 | $2,055 plus 12% of the amount over $20,550 |
| 22% | $83,551 to $178,150 | $9,615 plus 22% of the amount over $83,550 |
| 24% | $178,151 to $340,100 | $30,427 plus 24% of the amount over $178,150 |

| | | |
|---|---|---|
| 32% | $340,101 to $431,900 | $69,295 plus 32% of the amount over $340,100 |
| 35% | $431,901 to 647,850 | $98,671 plus 35% of the amount over $431,900 |
| 37% | $647851 or more | $174,253.50 plus 37% of the amount over $647,850 |

A common misconception among taxpayers is that if your taxable income falls in a certain tax bracket then all of your income is taxed in that bracket. That is not correct and here is an example of how tax would be calculated on taxable income of $200,000 which would fall in the 24 percent bracket:

| Description | Taxable Income | Tax Due |
|---|---|---|
| Tax at 10%, 12% & 22% | $178,150 | $30,427 |
| Tax at 24% | $21,850 | $5,244 |
| Total Tax Due | $200,000 | $35,671 |

So, as you can see, only a small portion ($21,850) of the $200,000 is actually taxed at the 24 percent rate; the balance of the income is taxed at lower rates as reflected in the tax rate schedule.

* * *

Taxpayers in the upper tax brackets can often save substantial tax dollars by *shifting income* to taxpayers in lower tax brackets than they are. There are many way to accomplish this. Here are some examples of how my clients have done it.

## *Your Kids on the Payroll*

If you have kids, and you own a business, even a small side-business, here is a fabulous learning opportunity for the kids and a tax-saving opportunity for you. This works best when your kids are under eighteen years old. Let me explain how it works:

Let's say your business is an S corporation and you want to hire your fourteen-year old to handle some social media projects for your business. You could have your S corporation hire your child directly, but then he would be treated like a normal employee. While there would be some tax benefit , doing it this way is not optimal. In order to be exempt from payroll taxes you need to have a direct parent-to- child relationship and having your S corporation in the middle doesn't work.

Here is our strategy for this situation:

- You establish a separate business as a sole-proprietor or

as a husband/wife partnership
- Your S corporation hires your separate business to do the social media project
- Your separate business hires your child to do the project

Doing it this way, you are exempt from paying the 15.3 percent payroll taxes on your childs wages. In most cases your child wouldn't even need to file a tax return. Your S corporation takes a tax deduction for the full amount paid for the project.

Obviously, your child actually needs to do the work and the amount you pay needs to be reasonable, but you can certainly pay what outside vendors would charge for similar work. Some years ago I had a client pay his fifteen-year-old son $20,000 for website development. His son, matched the lowest other bid we got.

Tax benefits aside, this is a great opportunity to teach your child about work. Perhaps consider replacing an allowance with wages?

## *Sale/Lease Back of Business Equipment*

So let's say you have a parent you would like to give some money to on a monthly basis to help them make ends meet.

Obviously, you could just give them money you have already paid tax on. But here is a strategy we have used for this situation that works well and can save a lot of taxes:

- Find all the equipment you use in your business that's been fully depreciated
- Do a sale/lease back agreement for the equipment with your parent. You can gift your parent the funds to complete the purchase of the equipment if necessary. It's likely the equipment is not worth much anyway

Your parent gets the monthly income for your lease payments, and your business takes a deduction for the payments. There are lots of variations of this strategy. Your tax advisor can help you structure something that works perfectly for you.

## Gift/Sale of Appreciated Property

As in the previous strategy, let's say you have a parent you want to give some money to to help them make ends meet. As before, you could just give them money you have already paid taxes on. But here is a strategy you may like better. Assuming you have some appreciated stock you want to sell, instead of selling the stock you gift it to your parent and let your parent sell the stock. By doing it this way, all the gain on the stock is *shifted* to your parent. If the value of the stock exceeds $15,000 you will need to do a gift tax return, but because of your lifetime credit you won't owe any tax.

Yes, your parent may need to pay some tax on this gain, but it should be a lot less than you would pay on the same gain.

## *Pay Your C Corporation*

In the event you don't have anyone you want to shift income to, you can use this strategy, which works especially well for very profitable businesses. Here is how it works:

First set up a C corporation to provide some necessary service for your business. Maybe it's marketing, IT or payroll, whatever is a good fit for your particular situation. Your business then makes tax-deductible payments to your C corporation for these services. As an example, let's say you pay $75,000 for various marketing activities and you're in the 37 percent tax bracket.

|  | Payments | Tax Rate | Tax |
| --- | --- | --- | --- |
| Tax Saved by You | $75,000 | 37% | $27,750 |
| Tax Paid by C corp | $75,000 | 21% | ($15,750) |
| Net Tax Savings |  |  | $12,000 |

You may be wondering what happens to the funds remaining in the C corporation after the tax payment. They can be loaned to your business for expansion or perhaps to an investment company that you own to finance an investment.

# CHAPTER FOUR

## Convert Income

### *Income Types*

From a tax prospective, all income is not created equal. At times you can improve your tax situation by converting one type of income to another, but before I get into that, let's review the various types of income:

### *Earned Income*

From a tax perspective, earned income is often the worst type of income you can have. It's taxed at ordinary income rates plus FICA and Medicare taxes or self-employment taxes if the income is from self-employment. It can also be subject to a 3 percent Medicare surtax if your total income reaches a certain point. It should be noted that earned income is the only type of income you can use to qualify to make an IRA, pension or 401(k) contribution. Here is a tax rate breakdown:

| Tax Type | Rate |
|---|---|
| Ordinary Income | 10% - 37% |
| FICA/Medicare/Self-Employment | 15.3% |
| Medicare Surtax | 3% |
| Total Tax Rate | 25.3% - 55.3% |

## *Ordinary Income*

Ordinary income is all income that doesn't qualify as another type of income. It is taxed on a graduated basis depending on your taxable income at rates anywhere from 10 to 37 percent. A common conversion strategy is to convert earned income to ordinary income. You will see an example of this later in this chapter.

## *Investment or Portfolio Income*

Investment income is typically dividends and interest. Some investment income is taxable at ordinary income rates, but there are some very significant exceptions that *strategic taxpayers*™ can take advantage of. Warren Buffet once famously stated he pays a lower tax rate than his secretary. Obviously, Mr Buffet is a *strategic taxpayer*™. While his secretary has mostly earned income, his income is mostly dividends and capital gains which are taxed at much lower rates than earned income. The tax rates on qualified dividends and capital gains range from zero to 20 percent.

## *Passive Income*

Passive income comes from investing in passive activities. There are three common types as follows:

- Energy Oil & Gas
- Real Estate Rental
- Private Equity

I am going to go over energy and real estate investments in the chapter on tax deduction strategies so stay tuned. As for private equity, this is essentially where you invest in someone else's business. For example, let's say I become a 20 percent limited partner in a tax practice. I contribute cash, assets or intellectual property, but I don't do any actual work in the practice. My 20 percent of the profits from the practice will be passive income because someone else is doing all the work.

The great thing about passive income is that you can use passive losses to offset the income and make it non-taxable.

## *Qualified Business Income*

For tax years beginning after December 31, 2017 we have a new type of income that is used in calculating the qualified business income (QBI) deduction of up to 20 percent. I am going to cover QBI in the chapter on tax deduction strategies so I won't discuss it further here.

## *Typical Conversion Scenarios*

The following are examples of conversion strategies. Keep in mind, it is often possible to use multiple strategies in a given scenario, thereby generating tax savings on top of tax savings. Obviously, this can get very complicated so don't try any of these strategies without the help of a competent tax advisor.

## *Earned Income to S Corp Distribution*

Most small businesses in the United States are sole proprietorships, which is sad because I am sure that many of them are grossly overpaying their taxes. What's worse is, that this is a very easy problem to fix but most sole proprietors don't even know they have a problem. They just keep overpaying their taxes. Let's explore how the fix works:

All income from a sole proprietorship is earned income. If we set up an S corporation and have it take over the business, we can control and optimize the amount of earned income that is generated by setting the salary of the former sole proprietor. The remaining profit is converted to ordinary income and not subject to FICA and Medicare taxes. The salary needs to be reasonable I usually see around a third to a half of the earned income that was reported as a sole proprietor. On a $100,000 net profit business we usually see over $10,000 in tax savings from this strategy alone.

## *Ordinary Income to Passive Income*

Let's say we have a taxpayer with a successful business operating as an S corporation. The taxpayer has a parent that needs some additional income for monthly expenses etc. Of course the taxpayer could just gift the money out of post-tax income. But a better way would be to give some non-voting shares in the S corporation to the parent. Because the parent is not active in the business, all of the income received would be passive. If the parent had real estate or other passive losses they could be used to offset the passive income. A taxpayer can take this strategy further by also giving an interest a passive activity that the taxpayer controls that operates at a loss which would also offset the passive income.

## *Ordinary Income to Capital Gain*

Let's say you bought a fixer-upper about six months ago. You have completed all the repairs and upgrades and now you are ready to sell it. You got a great deal on the purchase so after all your costs you are expecting to net $100,000 profit. If you sell now you will be taxed at ordinary income rates. But if instead of selling you rent out the property for the next year you can substantially reduce your tax bill as follows:

| Description | Flip Sale | Rent Then Sell |
|---|---|---|
| Profit | $100,000 | $100,000 |
| Tax Due | $37,000 | $20,000 |
| Net After Tax | $63,000 | $80,000 |
| Tax Savings | ($17,000) | $17,000 |

# CHAPTER FIVE

## Defer Tax On Income

Strategies to defer taxes allow you to earn money today, but pay tax at some point in the future. These can certainly be helpful as a last resort, but I try to focus on strategies that will eliminate tax forever, not just temporarily. Unfortunately many taxpayers and even tax professionals erroneously believe that deferral is the only option available. Here are some deferral strategies we use frequently:

### *Qualified Retirement Plans*

Probably the most used form of tax deferral is the retirement plan. These come in many flavors so you have a lot of options, particularly if you are in business without any employees other than you and your spouse. Deductible contributions can range any where from zero to over $150,000 per year in the case of a Defined Benefit Plan. If you have employees and you set up a retirement plan you will need to cover your employees as well, the only exception is the IRA plan.

Setting up a retirement plan can be very complicated. Just about every plan can be established with many banks, credit unions, mutual funds, and of course stock brokerage firms. I strongly believe it will be in your best interest to work with your tax advisor *first* to review all of your options *before* you go to a bank or broker to establish the plan.

That being said, I am not going to take the time to outline all of your options because I'm sure it would put you to sleep.

Remember, this is just a deferral. The taxes you save today, will need to be paid sometime in the future. Some would argue that your tax bracket will be lower in the future, but I would not count on that being the case. At best, I would consider whatever you do with a qualified retirement plan to be just a small part of your overall wealth strategy which should focus on accumulating cash flow assets.

## Real Estate Exchange - IRC Sec. 1031

My favorite form of tax deferral is, without a doubt, the 1031 real estate exchange. If you own or plan to own investment real estate this is your new best friend.

What 1031 allows you to do is to exchange a real property you own for another real property and defer any taxes that would be otherwise due if you would have sold your property. Now you may be thinking how am I ever going to find someone with a property I want that also wants my property.

Well the good news is, you can actually do this like a conventional sale, but the escrow will be handled differently. This works in two ways depending on if the all the transactions can be closed simultaneously or if one or more transactions will be delayed.

As I'm sure you realize, this can get a bit complicated, so you need to make sure your real estate broker, tax advisor, and title company are very familiar with the process so everything goes as planned.

In order for your exchange to be completely tax deferred, it needs to pass the "Napkin Test," which was invented over a cocktail by California real estate attorney Marvin Starr. To pass the test you need be able to answer yes to the following questions:

\* \* \*

- Are you trading up in value?
- Are you trading equal or greater in equity?
- Are you trading up in mortgage?

If you are doing a delayed exchange you will need a qualified intermediary, who holds the cash after your property is sold and uses it to purchase your replacement property. You can't touch the funds or your exchange fails automatically. I strongly recommend you use only a bank, licensed trust company or title company as an intermediary. Once your property is sold there are some deadlines you must meet or your exchange will fail.

### *Forty-five-Day Rule*

Within forty-five days of the sale of your property, you must designate the replacement property in writing to the intermediary, specifying the property that you want to acquire. You can name up to three properties as long as you close on one of them.

### *180-Day Rule*

You must close on the new property within 180 days of the sale of the old property. Remember both these time periods run concurrently.

### *Reverse Exchange*

It is possible to acquire your replacement property before

selling your existing property and still qualify for a 1031 exchange. You will still need to comply with the forty-five day and 180-day rules.

## *Deferral Forever?*

As long as you keep exchanging you can defer tax indefinitely. You can also combine this strategy with a refi to generate tax-free cash. Keep in mind you can't do an exchange and a cash-out refi at the same time. I recommend you put at least twelve months between them.

## CHAPTER SIX

## Tax Deduction Strategies

Having a basic understanding of how tax deductions work is critical if you want to avoid overpaying your taxes. Start with the assumption that you are NOT deducting everything you can. I suggest you make a list of all the expenses you are not deducting. Then, discuss each of them with your tax advisor, I bet you will find some expenses you can deduct. You may be thinking you can skip this chapter and just rely on your tax advisor. That may be true if you're married to your tax advisor and you spend all your time together. However, most people are not spending near enough time with their tax advisor. The reality is that you make decisions everyday that will affect your tax situation for better or worse. All tax deductions arise out of legislative grace. That's a fancy way of saying that Congress can create tax deductions and prescribe rules governing usage. The good news is that everything you need to know about tax deductions is included in this chapter. Your tax advisor will help you with the details and make sure you get every deduction you are entitled to.

Tax deductions fall into three categories:
- Personal deductions
- Portfolio/investment deductions
- Business deductions

## Personal Deductions

Personal deductions relate to personal living expenses. But before we get in to some specifics let's review the standard deduction that every taxpayer gets automatically. Most personal deductions are what we call itemized deductions which are reported on Schedule A of form 1040. You would only claim your itemized deductions if the total amount exceeded your standard deduction; you don't get to claim both. You only pay tax on the income that exceeds the amount of your deductions, either itemized or standard. Here are the standard deduction amounts for 2022:

| Filing Status | Standard Deduction |
|---|---|
| Single, MFS | $12,950 |
| Married Filing Jointly | $25,900 |
| Head of Household | $19,400 |

## Home Mortgage Interest

You can deduct the mortgage interest you pay on your primary home and a second home as well. The deduction is limited to loans totaling up to $750.000. Obviously, renters don't get this deduction, so if you are currently renting a home or apartment, buying a home would be something you should talk to your tax advisor about.

## Taxes

Your deduction for taxes is now limited to a total of $10,000. Between state income taxes and real estate taxes many taxpayers will reach the limit. There may be some strategies to beat the limitation depending on where you live, check with your tax advisor.

## Charitable Contributions

Charitable deductions are often missed because taxpayers don't save receipts and a lot of donations are made spontaneously. I suggest you come up with a system to make sure all of your receipts are captured in one place. I am a big fan of online document management systems that allow you to scan and store your documents.

## Medical Expenses

I have very few clients that can deduct medical expenses on a personal basis. These expenses are deductible if they exceed 7.5

percent of your adjusted gross income. So if your adjusted gross was $100,000 you can deduct medical expenses that exceed $7,500.

| Adjusted Gross Income | $100,000 |
| Total Medical Expenses | $12,000 |
| Exclusion Amount | ($7,500) |
| Medical Expense Deduction | $4,500 |

There are much better options for deducting medical expenses as a business deduction, I will cover that later in this chapter.

## Portfolio/Investment Expenses

Under current law, many of these types of expenses are not deductible. This limitation is scheduled to end after 2025, but I would not bet on that happening. If you have major expenses in this area, you should review them with your tax advisor and determine how to get the most out of these expenses for tax purposes. The biggest impact for my clients is in the area of investment advisor fees, which can be substantial.

### *Investment Interest Expense*

When you borrow money to make an investment, the interest you pay can be a tax deduction. The most common use of this is margin loans which are obtained from a stockbroker. Your investment interest deduction is limited to the amount of your investment income. If your interest expense exceeds your income the remaining amount can be carried over to future years.

## *Business Expenses*

By the time you finish reading this chapter you will understand the incredible magic of business expense deductions. You will know why the wealthy typically own multiple businesses. One of my favorite billionaires, Richard Branson, owns more than six hundred businesses. But even one business, done correctly will save you big money on your taxes. So let's dive in!

One of the great things about business deductions, is there are few limitations. Yes there are certain expenses that the code says are not deductible, but those are few and far between. The reality is most any expense can be a business deduction under the right circumstances. Let's review the three guidelines that qualify an expense as a business deduction:

- **Business Purpose** - this means that the primary reason for the expense must be related to your business. Yes, there can be non-business purposes too but they need to be incidental.
- **Ordinary** - this means that the expense is typical in your

type of business

- **Necessary** - this means you believe the expense will help your business be more profitable

So when you are contemplating an expense, the question to ask your tax advisor is, "How can I make this expense a business deduction?" Keep in mind, you will get better results if you ask that question before you incur the proposed expense. Tax strategy is about your future, not your past.

## *How To Make an Expense Deductible*

Let's say you are a real estate agent from Las Vegas and you would like to go spend a few days on Maui. How can that be deductible? Well you need to do three things:

- **Establish a business purpose** - you are going to Maui to meet with other real estate agents to set up referral opportunities and explore the market for rental opportunities
- **Make sure the expense in ordinary** - as a prudent business owner your travel expenses will be reasonable and consistent with your income and circumstances. Most real estate agents would not charter a corporate jet to make this trip, so you should fly commercial. But you can fly first class if you like.

- **Make sure the expense is necessary** - setting up referral partners and looking for rental property opportunities is very likely to increase your profit in your real estate business

Now that we have covered the basics of how tax deductions work, we are going to dive deeper and go over some specific tax deductions starting with my absolute favorite which is depreciation.

## Depreciation & Amortization

In order to encourage business owners and investors to purchase fixed assets which creates jobs and builds our economy, Congress has given us the magic of depreciation and amortization. Both these deductions are conceptually similar. We use depreciation when we purchase tangible property, like real estate or equipment. But we use amortization when we purchase intangible property like a customer list, patents, trademarks and domain names.

### *How Depreciation Works*

When you buy an asset for your business or for the production of income you get to deduct a portion of it each year you own it. Let's look at an example:

I purchased an office condo to use for our office on Maui. Every year I get to take a depreciation deduction of around $15,000. Now I can assure you, the value of the condo is NOT going down, but for tax purposes I get to pretend it is. So I get a significant tax deduction without incurring any actual expense. Isn't that like having your cake and eating it too?

## *How Amortization Works*

Amortization works like depreciation except it's used when we purchase intangible property, for example. I have a client that purchased a domain name for his business. The cost was $250,000. My client can take an amortization deduction of $16,667 for the next fifteen years. My client is using the domain name to make money in his business and he expects the name to be worth more than what he paid for it in the coming years. Like with depreciation, my client is getting a tax deduction without giving up any value.

## Deduct Personal Expenses

Wouldn't it be great to be able to take a tax deduction for expenses you are already paying every month but you're not able to deduct them? Well if you have a business you can do just that.

If you don't have a business, you should start one soon because with every passing day you're losing more deductions. Let's review some of the strategies we use to turn personal expenses into business deductions.

## *Accountable Plans*

The best way to handle expense reimbursements for you and/or other employees of your business is to use an accountable plan. Using such a plan gives you three great benefits:

- You don't need to pay payroll taxes on the payments
- The reimbursement payments are not taxable income to you or your employee
- Your business can deduct the full amount of the reimbursement payment

Payments to you or your employees can be made through advanced payments, charges to your business credit card, billings to your business and of course direct reimbursements.

In order for a plan to qualify it must meet the following requirements:

- Payment recipients must provide proper documentation

- for claimed expenses
- Recipients must return any excess payments to the business

The plan is not required to be in writing, but if you have employees other than family, putting the plan in writing is strongly recommended. See your tax advisor for help with all the details.

## *Business Travel & Meals*

When you travel overnight for a business purpose the tax law allows you to deduct your expenses, such as airfare, hotel bills, meals and other costs. With a little planning, you can combine business with pleasure and still take a tax deduction. It should be noted that travel deductions are frequently subject to IRS audit, so it's very important to follow the rules and document all of your expenses.

In order to be deductible the primary purpose of your trip must be business and you must have a business intent and purpose before leaving on your trip. Here are some examples of business purpose:

- Searching for new customers or clients

- Investigating your competition
- Meeting with existing customers or clients
- Meeting with people that could help your business such as investors
- Learning new skills related to your business

It's not enough to just claim you had a business purpose for your trip, you need to be able to prove you spent significant time engaged in business activities while at your destination. Some acceptable business activities would include all of the following:

- Visiting existing or potential clients or customers
- Attending a convention or trade show related to your business
- Attending an educational seminar related to your business
- Meeting with people that could help your business such as investors

Keep in mind you can count the whole day as a business day as long as you spend at least four hours engaged in business activities; the rest of your time can be spent on non-business activities of your choice, like relaxing by the pool etc.

It's best if at least some of your business activities can be arranged before you begin your trip. I suggest reaching out to the people you are planning to meet to schedule time. Obviously, any written documentation you have of this pre-planning will clearly establish your business purpose for the trip

I think you can see from this brief overview there is a lot of opportunity to combine business and personal travel. While it probably won't work for your honeymoon trip, most any other trip can be planned and conducted in a way that will meet all the rules so the trip will be tax-deductible

## *Medical Expense Reimbursement*

You have probably noticed, the cost of health insurance and medical care in general just keeps rising with each passing day. Wouldn't it be great if you could deduct the cost of medical insurance and all your other medical bills as business expenses? Well you can, if your business sets up a Medical Expense Reimbursement Plan, also known as a Section 105 Plan

Like all employee benefit plans, all participants need to qualify as employees. This can present a problem for many small business owners because in most cases they are considered self-employed and hence don't qualify as an employee. There are some strategies to make the business owner eligible as follows:

| Owner Eligibility ||
|---|---|
| Business Entity Type | How to Get Coverage |
| Sole Proprietorship | Hire Spouse |
| Partnership | Hire Spouse (if <5% owner) |
| S Corporation | 2% Shareholders Ineligible |
| C Corporation | Hire Yourself |

In many cases when the medical expenses are significant I will setup a C corporation to operate some part of the business and then employ the owner so he or she is eligible. This strategy works well for businesses without employees outside the owner's family. Because all eligible employees need to be covered, if your business has non-family employees this may not be practical for you. However, it is possible to exclude certain employees from coverage as follows:

- Employees under age twenty-five
- Employees working less than thirty-five hours per week
- Employees working less than nine months per year
- Employees with less than three years' tenure
- Employees covered by a collective bargaining agreement

The rules in this area are very complicated. But your tax

advisor can work with you to develop a strategy that gives you the best possible benefit in your situation.

## *Home Office Reimbursement*

If you own a business you will want to establish an office in your home. This is true whether you own or rent your place of residence. The benefits of having a home office are substantial and easy to qualify for. Here is a quick overview of the rules:

- You have a business
- You use your home office exclusively for business
- You use your home office on a regular basis

If you answered yes to all of the above you qualify for a home office if you meet any one of the following requirements:

- Your home office is your primary place of business
- You meet customers or clients in your home office
- You store product samples or inventory in your home
- You operate a day care center at home
- You use a separate building on your property exclusively for business purposes
- You use your home office regularly and exclusively for administrative and management tasks for your business and have no other fixed location where you do such tasks

\* \* \*

You will note, for a sole proprietor, home office expense is a deduction which is claimed on form 8829. When a business is operated through a corporation, partnership or other entity the business owner is reimbursed for the office expenses under an accountable plan as described earlier in this chapter. Of course the business entity will take a tax deduction for the reimbursement.

## *Calculating Your Home Office Reimbursement*

The first step is to determine how much of your home is being used for your business as a percentage. The IRS publication on this topic suggests you use the gross square footage method. However, I typically use the net square footage method because it yields a higher percentage of business use in most cases. I have an Excel sheet that I have my clients complete to do this calculation. You can download a copy of this Excel sheet along with many other resources on the website for this book at www.strategictaxpayer.com/resources.

## *What Expenses Can You Include?*

As I am sure you know, you incur a lot of expenses operating your home. The good news is ALL of them can be included in your reimbursement calculation. Let's review how the calculation works.

First of all there are two categories of expenses:

- Direct Expenses - these are expenses that just apply to your home office not the rest of your home. For example let's say you had carpet installed in your home office or maybe you had some better lighting installed over your desk or maybe you paid someone to clean your office. All of these expenses are 100 percent reimbursable.
- Indirect Expenses - these are expenses that benefit your entire home, both the business and personal use areas. You may only claim a portion of this expense, the home office percentage of the total is reimbursable.

Most of my clients do their home office reimbursements on a monthly basis but you can do it less often if you like. I suggest you work with your tax advisor to put together a home office expense report in Excel that you can do each month to document the expenses and then do the reimbursement. I have included some sample expense reports on the website you will find at www.strategictaxpayer.com/resources

Another great benefit to having a home office relates to your business auto expenses. Because with a home office you can start and finish your business day at home you eliminate non-deductible commuting expense. I will be covering auto expenses next.

\* \* \*

## *Business Auto Expense*

Being able to drive a nice car that your business pays for is a beautiful thing. Getting a big tax deduction as a part of the deal is like icing on the cake. Let's review some things you need to know in order to make the most out of this opportunity.

First of all, you're probably best off if you own your car personally rather than have your business own it, because the insurance and finance cost will be much higher with your business as the owner. Owning is also most likely better than leasing as well. You will get the best results from a tax prospective if you use your car more than 50 percent for business use. This should be pretty easy if you have a home office, because you will likely be able to combine some personal use with business use, such as stopping at the store to buy groceries on your way home from a business call.

Because you own your car you will need to submit expense reports to your business under your business' accountable plan. Your business can then reimburse you for your expenses. Of course, your business can pay your auto expenses directly as well as long as everything is reconciled with your accountable plan.

You will need to track your business vs personal use and there are many ways to do it. Take a look at the smart phone apps that do most of the work for you via GPS.

I suggest you meet with your tax advisor to review your auto use and determine how to best maximize your reimbursements. Keep in mind you can use more than one car in your business; just make sure your business use exceeds 50 percent on each vehicle to maximize your deduction and reimbursement opportunities.

## *Athletic Facilities*

Your business can provide a gym or other athletic facility on your business premises for the use of your employees and their families, including you and your family. If your business premises are at your home you can have your athletic facilities there as well. I have clients who have used this provision to deduct swimming pool maintenance, putting greens, and of course exercise gyms. For more information on this see IRC Sec 132(j)(4).

## Tax Incentivized Activities

In chapter one I wrote about Congress using the tax code to encourage taxpayers to do certain things it thinks are of benefit to society. A great example of this would be home ownership. That's why we can deduct home mortgage interest and why there are incentives for first-time home buyers.

Now I am going to review several activities that Congress has made extremely attractive from both a tax and an economic perspective.

## *Real Estate Investment*

My favorite investment is real estate, for two reasons, 1)debt and 2)depreciation. It's like magic, you can purchase a $500,000 property with only $100,000 down and a $400,000 mortgage. You can then claim depreciation on the entire purchase price less the land value. In other words, you get to claim depreciation on the bank's money not just the cash you put in. So by using debt you're not only leveraging your return on investment, you are also leveraging you tax benefits.

I have many clients with substantial monthly income from real estate that is entirely tax-free. Imagine how good you would feel if all of your living expenses were covered by tax-free income from your real estate portfolio. That can be your reality and leverage and tax incentives will help you get there.

Real estate investments generate passive income or passive losses. Passive income is generally a good thing, but passive losses can normally only be deducted against passive income which can sometimes be a challenge-which is why we are always looking for ways to create more passive income. There are a couple of exceptions to this rule that I will cover a little later.

Another great benefit available only with real estate, is the tax-deferred exchange I wrote about in chapter five. I strongly suggest that you talk with your tax advisor and see how you can incorporate real estate investments into your tax and wealth strategy.

## *Active Participant*

If you actively participate in a real estate rental activity you can deduct up to $25,000 in real estate losses as active losses. These active losses can offset any type of income. To take advantage of this exception from the passive loss rules your adjusted gross income must be less than $100,000. If your AGI exceeds $100,000 the deduction is phased out at a rate of two dollars for every dollar exceeding $100,000 as shown in the table below.

| Adjusted Gross Income | Maximum Loss Allowed |
| --- | --- |
| <= $100,000 | $25,000 |
| $125,000 | $12,500 |
| >= $150,000 | 0 |

## *Qualified Real Estate Professional*

Another exemption from the passive loss rules is available for real estate professionals. While real estate agents, building contractors and other professionals in the real estate business generally qualify as real estate professionals you can also qualify if you meet all of the following:

- Work at least 750 hours per year in the real estate business
- Own at least 10 percent of the real estate business
- Spend more time working in the real estate business than all other business activities combined.

Being able to treat real estate losses as active losses is a tremendous advantage. One the strategies I have used with my clients is to have a non-working spouse take charge of managing the family real estate portfolio. This works well if the family has at least three properties. I suppose it can be done with less but you would need to carefully document the 750 hours of work in the business.

## *Cost Segregation*

Assuming you have a lot of passive income or you qualify as a real estate professional, you can supercharge your depreciation deduction by doing a cost segregation study on your rental or business use property. Normally when you place real property in service you do an allocation of land and improvements. Because land does not deteriorate you can't claim depreciation on it. But the improvements can be depreciated over 27.5 years for residential property or 39 years for non-residential property.

With a cost segregation study, a professional engineer does a breakdown of the improvements to various components. Some components will have shorter lives than the structure and can be depreciated faster. See the tables below for example:

| $500,000 Property Without Cost Segregation |||
|---|---|---|
| Description | Cost | Annual Depreciation |
| Land | $100,000 | 0 |
| Improvements 27.5-yr life | $400,000 | $14,545 |
| Total Depreciation || $14,545 |

| $500,000 Property With Cost Segregation |||
|---|---|---|
| Description | Cost | Annual Depreciation |
| Land | $75,000 | 0 |
| Land Improve. 15-yr life | $25,000 | $1,667 |
| Personal Property 7-yr life | $50,000 | $7,143 |
| Personal Property 5-yr life | $50,000 | $10,000 |
| Structure 27.5-yr life | $300,000 | $10,909 |
| Total Depreciation || $29,719 |

* * *

Obviously, the best time to do a cost segregation is when you first place a property in service. But it's possible to use a cost segregation to go back catch up on all the deductions you missed even if you placed the property in service many years ago. These missed deductions can be taken in a single year by filing form 3115 with your tax return.

## *Oil & Gas Investment*

Oil and gas is the only passive investment you can make that is exempt from the passive loss rules. If you invest in the correct way you can deduct your losses from oil and gas against your ordinary income even though your investment is completely passive.

The oil and gas investments with significant tax benefits are of two types and both are investments in actual drilling operations. The first is exploratory drilling also called "wildcat" drilling. This can be very risky, because there is no guarantee that they will find oil in the ground they are drilling. The second is called developmental drilling. Here they are drilling in established oil fields with proven reserves. This is less risky, but you can still lose your investment in these deals as well.

The major tax benefits of oil and gas are from intangible

drilling cost and depletion.

Intangible drilling cost is money that is spent drilling the wells. If you invest $100,000 into a drilling deal you should get 70 to 80 percent of your investment as a tax deduction in the first year.

If you have a productive well you can take a 15 percent depletion allowance every year based on the well's gross income, kind of like depreciation, but it never runs out as long as the well is producing.

Obviously, there is a lot more to oil and gas investment than I can cover here. These investments are not for everybody. If you think such an investment might be a good fit for you, I suggest you talk to your tax advisor and perhaps your investment advisor as well.

## *Create Intellectual Property*

If you are feeling creative, this might be just the thing for you. Probably the best examples of this would be movie production or software development. But a lot of activities fall into this category. Such as what I am doing now, writing a book.

I have had clients that invested in movie production, but most of my clients have been involved in creating software, books or educational training programs or other forms IP.

The big advantage here is you can spend time and money now

creating your intellectual property and all you spend is a business deduction. Then you can sell or license your IP on an ongoing basis. In other words, create it once, but sell it many times.

## *Opportunity Zone*

The Tax Cuts and Jobs Act created the Opportunity Zones tax incentive. This economic development tool allows taxpayers to invest in distressed areas called opportunity zones. The biggest benefit to opportunity zone investment is being able to defer an eligible capital gain. For example, let's say a you have a $200,000 gain on some google stock you sold, if you invest that gain in a Qualified Opportunity Fund your gain can be deferred until there is an event that reduces or terminates your investment in the fund or December 31, 2026, which ever is earlier.

I am generally not a big fan of deferral unless that is the only option. I expect the big problem will be finding a quality investment located in an Opportunity Zone.

If this sounds like something you would be interested in, be sure to bring your tax advisor in on the proposed deal early in the game to make sure everything is structured correctly.

## Charitable Deduction Strategies

If you are like me, giving money to a worthy cause always

makes you feel good. So much the better when such generosity saves big money on your taxes. Let's review a few strategies that my clients have used to supercharge their charitable deductions.

## *Donate Appreciated Property*

Let's say you want to donate $10,000 to your favorite university. Of course you could just write a check and you would get a nice tax deduction. However, donating some appreciated stock that you bought for $3,000 and is now worth $10,000 might be a better option. Let's compare:

| Description | Donate Cash | Donate Stock |
| --- | --- | --- |
| Donation amount | $10,000 | $10,000 |
| Tax savings | $3,700 | $3,700 |
| Capital gain avoided |  | $1,400 |
| Total Tax Savings | $3,700 | $5,100 |

So you save an extra $1,400 by donating the stock, and if you like that stock you can buy $10,000 worth with the cash you would have donated. But now your basis in the stock will be $10,000.

## *Charitable Remainder Trust*

In most cases, you make a charitable gift, you get a tax deduction and you are done. A charitable remainder trust (CRT) acts like a gift with strings attached allowing you continuing benefits from your gift. CRTs are generally used when you are selling a major asset at a large gain and you want to avoid paying taxes. If your deal and CRT are structured correctly your tax savings can actually outweigh the amount you are giving away. Obviously, this is a complicated arrangement, but the gist of it is you can receive income from the trust for a period of time even for life. And at the end of the prescribed income period the remainder is left to the charity. You get a current tax deduction for the present value of the remainder interest per IRS rules. If this sounds like something you could benefit from you should consult your tax advisor before entering in to an agreement to sell the asset(s) in question.

## *Charitable Lead Trust*

The charitable lead trust (CLT) is similar to the charitable remainder trust except the beneficiary roles are reversed. In the CLT income is paid to the charity for a period of time then at the end the remainder goes back to you. You get a current tax deduction for the present value of the income interest per IRS rules. If this sounds like something you could benefit from you should consult your tax advisor.

## Donor Advised Fund

Many investment brokerages are now offering a charitable giving account called a donor advised fund. This acts like a brokerage account but it's dedicated to charity. You get an immediate tax deduction for contributions. These funds can be invested for growth and you can recommend donations to any IRS-qualified public charity. This option is considerably less expensive than setting up your own charity or foundation.

## Private Foundations

If you would like more control over your charitable contributions or you can't find a current charity that supports your cause or causes, setting up a private foundation may be your answer.

A private foundation, like a public charity or public foundation, is organized to carry out a charitable mission. The main difference is that a private foundation is funded and controlled by an individual, family or perhaps a corporation. Just like a public charity, donors get a tax deduction for contributions. Unlike public charities, private foundations are required to pay an excise tax of 1.39 percent on net investment income. If you plan to devote a significant portion of your wealth to charitable purposes this is probably how you should do it. The rules in this area are very complicated, so make sure your tax advisor has experience in this area or get a referral to someone that does.

## *Conservation Easements*

With a conservation easement, taxpayers can get a charitable deduction for agreeing not to develop land they own. Unfortunately there has been a lot of abusive transactions in this area so these transactions are on the IRS's "HIT list" and are frequently audited and disallowed. While some taxpayers have successfully defended their transactions in the end I doubt it was economically profitable considering litigation expenses.

The abuse comes in to play in establishing the value of the conservation easement. For example, against my advice, one of my clients put $20,000 into a conservation easement deal and received a charitable deduction of $80,000. I told my client to plan on being audited; I am sure the IRS will see this as abusive. My client believes the transaction is defensible. We shall see?

While I believe that conservation easements can benefit taxpayers, extreme care needs to be exercised to avoid over valuation and all the problems that come with it.

## Qualified Business Income

The Tax Cuts and Jobs Act (TCJA) passed at the end of 2017 lowered the tax rate for C corporations to a flat 21 percent. The problem that Congress was facing in getting the bill passed was that most US businesses are not C corporations and would not benefit from the lower rate. As a point of fairness, Congress added the qualified business income deduction to the TCJA.

The qualified business income deduction is a 20 percent deduction for income that an individual taxpayer receives from a pass-through business, such as a partnership or S corporation. Sole proprietorships are also eligible.

Taking this deduction can be complicated and there are income limitations that can reduce or eliminate the deduction altogether. But it should be noted that in 2018 the Inspector General for Tax Administration found almost 900,000 tax returns that didn't claim the deduction but appeared to qualify for it. Don't let this happen to you. See your tax advisor to make sure you are taking advantage of this deduction if you can.

# CHAPTER SEVEN

## Tax Credits

In the previous chapter I gave you an overview of many of the tax deductions that I see in my practice on a regular basis. In this chapter I am going to review some tax credits that my clients take advantage of. While deductions and credits are similar, credits are much better. So before I cover some actual credits, lets review the major difference between a deduction and a credit.

If you have a $10,000 tax deduction the amount of tax you save will depend on your marginal tax bracket. So if you are in the 35 percent tax bracket, a $10,000 deduction will save you $3,500 in tax.

With a tax credit your tax bracket does not matter because a $10,000 tax credit will save you $10,000 in tax. Some credits, such as the earned income credit are what we call "refundable." These credits will be paid to you even if you don't owe any tax.

Otherwise, with a nonrefundable credit, your unused credit is carried over to future tax years until you use it completely

There are three types of credits:

- Personal credits
- Investment credits
- Business credits

The most common personal credits are as follows:

- Child under 17 credit
- Dependent care credit
- Earned income credit
- First-time home buyer credit
- Health insurance credit
- Education credits
- Adoption credits

The most common investment credits are as follow:

- Low-income housing credit
- Wind power generation credit
- Solar energy credit
- Historic restoration credit
- Oil recovery credit

The most common business credits are as follows:

- Research and development credit
- New market credit
- Employment credit

- Employee retention credit (COVID-19- related)
- Employee health insurance credit
- Pension plan start-up credit

A word of caution! Failure to claim all the tax credits you are entitled to is probably the biggest missed opportunity facing taxpayers today. Frankly, no one at the IRS is going to care if you miss a big tax credit and overpay your taxes. It is up to you and your tax advisor to get this right and make sure you claim all the credits you are entitled to.

I strongly suggest you review the above list of credits with your tax advisor and determine which credits will be of benefit to you. I have a more comprehensive list of available tax credits on the website for this book at www.strategictaxpayer.com/resources

# CHAPTER EIGHT

## Entities Explained

There are several types of entities I work with on a regular basis in my practice. But before I cover the entities in detail I want to review some important concepts that you need to understand. First of all there are legal entities and there are tax entities. Legal entities are organized and governed under state law. Each state has different rules regarding entities. Here is a list legal entities available in most states.

- Individual
- Trust
- General partnership
- Limited partnership
- Limited Liability Company
- Corporation

Tax entities are based on federal law, not state law. You will notice, the list is a little different. Here is a list of tax entities:

- Individual
- Trust
- General partnership
- Limited partnership
- C corporation
- S corporation

So keep in mind, my review of entities is mainly from a tax prospective. Various legal aspects may be different depending on what state you are in.

## *Individual*

An individual is a person and normally we don't recommend doing business or holding assets as an individual, except on a limited basis such as your home, cars and personal financial accounts. There is usually a better way to operate from a tax and asset protection standpoint.

## *Sole Proprietorship*

When you operate a business as an individual it's called a sole proprietorship. Sadly most businesses in the United States are sole proprietorships and most are overpaying their taxes (if they are profitable) and taking financial risks that could easily be avoided. While there are situations when a sole proprietorship is appropriate, they are few and far between. FYI sole proprietorships are about twelve times more likely to be audited by the IRS than any other entity. I think that's reason enough not to be a sole proprietorship.

## *Trust*

A trust is really just a contract between the grantor and the trustee. The most common type of trust I see is a living trust which is frequently used to avoid probate upon the death of the grantor. Such a trust can be a good substitute for a will, although most people with a living trust will also have a will. A living trust is a revokable trust and is generally a disregarded entity for tax purposes which means all income or deductions for the trust would be reported on the tax return of the grantor.

Special types of irrevocable trusts can be established for estate planning and asset protection purposes. I wrote about two of these in chapter five. These trusts generally file their own tax returns but often will pass income and deductions on to beneficiaries for reporting on their tax returns.

Some states have what is called a business trust, but frankly, I have never encountered a situation where it made sense to use a trust to operate a business.

Lastly, a trust I have seen a lot of recently is the Delaware Statutory Trust. This trust is becoming very popular as vehicle to hold title to real estate for the benefit of multiple owners

## *Partnership*

If I had a favorite entity type it would be a partnership because it is undoubtedly the entity with the most flexibility. In reality, I don't have a favorite because I choose the type of entity based on the circumstances and no entity type is right for every situation. Often times I may use more than one type of entity to accomplish a result for a client. But I will get into that later in the chapter.

Partnerships come in two flavors a general partnership and a limited partnership. Both types file the same tax form but there are some major differences.

## *General Partnership*

A general partnership happens when two or more entities (including individuals) join together in business. You can start a general partnership with a handshake or you can have a 100-page partnership agreement. So the big advantage is they are easy and cheap to get started and maintain. The downside to a general partnership is everybody involved has unlimited liability. For this reason, I only use a general partnership when I am certain that liability is not a concern. As I covered in chapter three when I use a husband/wife partnership to employ their kids in a business activity.

## *Limited Partnership*

A limited partnership is more complicated from a paperwork perspective as partnership documents need to be filed with the state and fees paid etc. Also, most states require a written limited partnership agreement. Even with the complexity limited partnerships have some great advantages, the first being limited liability. There are two basic types of partners as follows:

A general partner has unlimited liability and is normally responsible for day-to-day management of the partnership. Of course there can be more than one general partner. How and by who the partnership is managed is generally spelled out in the partnership agreement As I mentioned, a general partner has unlimited liability, which is not good. But it is an easy problem to fix by using an entity that has limited liability as the general partner.

A limited partner has limited liability and is not involved in day-to-day management of the partnership. One of the great things about a limited partnership is you can have different classes of partners and the rights and responsibilities of each can vary by class. This is a great way to maintain control without owning all the equity in the partnership.

I will often use a limited partnership instead of an LLC (Limited Liability Company) in California because California has an LLC tax that is based on gross receipts that can be almost $12,000 per year. I have several clients that are saving over $10,000 each year because they are operating as a limited partnership instead of an LLC.

## *Corporation*

For tax purposes corporations come in two flavors a C corporation and a S corporation. While they are both the same from a legal perspective, they couldn't be more different from a tax perspective. Let's explore the advantages and disadvantages of each.

## *C Corporation*

A C corporation is a tax-paying entity. Most of the companies listed on the stock exchanges are C corporations. Under the Tax Cuts & Jobs Act C corporations pay a flat tax of 21 percent, which sounds pretty good if your personal tax bracket happens to be higher. The problem with C corporation is there is potential to pay double tax if you're not careful. You see the dividends paid by a C corporation to it's shareholders are not tax-deductible, but they are taxable income to the receiving shareholder. The C corporations I work with rarely pay dividends for that reason. C corporations do have a place in closely held business tax strategy. But a C corporation should only be used with the help of an experienced tax advisor.

## S Corporation

Many US small businesses are taxed as S corporations, and for good reason. An S corporation is the tried-and-true way to lower your FICA and Medicare tax burden as I discussed in chapter four.

So the big difference between a C corporation and a S corporation is that the S corporation is taxed like a partnership in that it is a passthrough entity. That means that net income is "passed through" to shareholders and the shareholders pay tax on the income at their personal tax rate.

It should be noted, that S corporations are not nearly as flexible as a partnership, because everything must be allocated to shareholders based on their percentage of stock.

Just about every tax strategy I do involves at least one S corporation, so I bet there is an S corporation in your future, if you don't already have one.

\* \* \*

## *Limited Liability Company*

I bet your wondering if I had a reason for covering the LLC last? Remember, LLCs were not on the list of tax entities. That because an LLC can choose to be taxed as any of the following entities:

- Individual
- Sole proprietorship
- Partnership
- S corporation
- C corporation

This makes LLCs incredibly flexible. Here is how it works. If an LLC has only one member it is disregarded for tax purposes. We don't use that very much for individual taxpayers but a partnership or a corporation can be a single member of an LLC for liability protection. A single member LLC can elect to be an S corporation; in fact many of my clients are LLCs taxed as S corporations. Make sure to discuss your LLC plans with your tax advisor so you can select the best tax entity for your purpose.

## *Choice of Entity*

Choosing the right entities to involve in your business and

financial life is absolutely critical to minimizing your taxes and your overall success. Every strategy engagement I do starts with drawing a diagram of all of the client's entities and what purposes they serve in my client's life. Often just by restructuring the entities involved I can save the client thousands of dollars. Many times the best entity for a given business enterprise is not just one entity but several. A good example would be my practice. The practice is organized as a limited partnership but me and my partners are all LLCs taxed as S corporations. The practices information technology functions are all handled by an LLC taxed as C corporation and the website and marketing is done by an LLC taxed as a partnership. Yes, a little complicated, but well worth the trouble in the long run. Don't wait to review your entity structure with your tax advisor and find out if you can make it serve you better. You can download my how-to guide to drawing entity diagrams on the book's website at www.strategictaxpayer.com/resources.

# CHAPTER NINE

## Tax Advisors

If you have read the preceding chapters in this book you should have a deep understanding of how important your tax advisor is in helping you pay the least amount of tax. Unfortunately the knowledge and experience of tax professionals varies significantly. In many states, you can hang your shingle and start preparing tax returns and advising taxpayers with no training at all. Even in the states that require training and testing, it can be done in less than 100 hours. One big reason for this is that the complexity of tax situations also varies widely. If all you have is a W2 and mortgage, just about anybody can prepare your tax return. But let's face it, nobody gets wealthy with just a W2 and a mortgage.

The more you have going on in your business and financial life, the better your tax advisor needs to be. Most tax advisors are experts in the 1 percent of the Internal Revenue Code that raises taxes. But very few are experts in the 99 percent of the code that reduces taxes.

## How Much Does Your Tax Advisor Cost You?

Some tax advisors will charge a low fee and you might think you're saving money. But if you're overpaying your taxes, that advisor could be costing you a lot more than you think. For example, last year I started working with a client that had been with their prior advisor for ten years. At my suggestion, the first thing we did was an entity strategy. My fee for the strategy was $10,000. One part of the strategy I designed was to convert the business from an LLC to a limited partnership. That one strategy saves the client more than $10,000 each year. The sad part of this story is the client could have done this ten years sooner and saved over $100,000 in taxes. So the reality is, the prior advisor actually cost $100,000 more than the fees they billed. The *strategic taxpayer*™ understands that a good tax advisor's fees are an investment not an expense.

## Tax Planning vs. Tax Strategy

Many tax professionals will say they do tax planning. But really what they do is take your numbers and do an estimate of what you are going to owe in taxes. Perhaps they will advise you to make some year-end purchases or contribute to a pension plan. When you ask what you can do to reduce your taxes, most of the advice you get will be around deferral. Occasionally, a tax professional will tell you can save on your taxes by making less money. If you ever hear that advice, you should turn around and run, because that's the dumbest advice you will ever hear.

Working with a tax strategist is very different. First of all, your strategist is going to ask a lot of questions to really get a complete understanding of your facts and circumstances. Your strategist will discuss your goals and give you feedback on what needs to happen to make your goals a reality. Next your strategist will consider everything I have written about in this book and determine what strategies are a good fit for your unique situation. Obviously, the ultimate strategy is a moving target so you should be meeting with your tax strategist on a quarterly basis at least.

## *Your Tax Advisor Options*

Here is a list of your tax advisor options:
- CPA - Certified Public Accountant
- Enrolled Agent
- Attorney
- Do-it-yourself
- Storefront - Mass Market Tax Preparer

So when it comes to tax advisors an absolute must is the ability to represent you before the tax agencies. If your advisor is not authorized to do this, you are at a considerable disadvantage.

While there are rare exceptions when it's appropriate, it's almost NEVER in your best interest to personally engage with any tax agency. Because the last two options can't represent you I am going to summarily dismiss them. So let's review the top three.

## CPA - Certified Public Accountant

Of all tax professionals, the CPA is probably the most well-known. CPA's are licensed by the state they practice in, so education and experience requirements vary from state to state. The training most CPAs get in school focuses on accounting principles and auditing, with only one or two tax courses being required. The CPA exam only has a very small section devoted to tax. However, many CPAs have done extensive training in tax and are experts. But just don't assume that because someone is a CPA they are a tax expert.

## Enrolled Agent

Enrolled Agents are less well-know as tax professionals than CPAs. Enrolled Agents are licensed by the US Treasury Department through the IRS. While there are no specific educational requirements to take the Enrolled Agent exam, the exam is very comprehensive and is just about taxes. Last I looked, the average passing rate was around 30 percent, so the exam is not easy. You need a pretty good understanding of tax law to successfully pass the exam.

## *Attorney*

Attorneys as a group are probably the most educated of all tax professionals. However there is no guarantee that any of that education was about taxes. So one should expect that an attorney in the tax business should have a master's degree or be a certified specialist. If you engage an attorney as your tax strategist, make sure that they actually prepare tax returns as a regular part of their practice. Hands-on experience is necessary for the best results.

From a practice prospective, attorneys do have one advantage that other tax professionals don't and that is attorney-client privilege. However, most taxpayers will never need or benefit from that.

## *Knowledge, Experience & Mindset*

I have spent a lot of time working with tax professionals from all of the above categories. I have found that it's not the credential that matters. In the making of a tax strategist here is what counts:

## *Knowledge*

Most tax professionals are experts on the 1 percent of the Internal Revenue Code that raises taxes, but you need a tax advisor that is also an expert on the 99 percent of the Code that reduces taxes. Certainly your tax advisor should be very familiar with all the concepts I have written about in this book. They should be able to explain in detail what you need to do to implement any of the strategies. A good tax advisor is always learning and looking for ways to gain new skills.

## *Experience*

As your guide, your tax advisor should have a complete understanding of the path you are on and what it is going take to get you to your destination. There is no substitute for direct experience. However don't confuse time with experience. Some will have thirty years experience, where others will have one year of experience repeated thirty times. The best indicator of experience is the questions they ask, because if they really understand the path you're on, the questions will be incredibly relevant and thought-provoking.

## *Mindset*

Your tax advisor's mindset is critical. Your advisor should be constantly looking for ways to improve your results. Your advisor's primary focus is always on creating the future you want. You advisor should strive to help you find clarity around your goals and what you need to accomplish them.

## *Working With a Tax Strategist*

Having read this book to this point, you should be well prepared to sit down with a tax strategist and start developing your tax strategy. Keep in mind, it's your tax strategy. Your tax advisor is merely your guide and counselor. Your first task should be to find clarity around all of the following:

- Where you are now from a tax and financial prospective
- Where you want to go
- How do you plan to get there
- Who needs to be involved in the process

# CHAPTER TEN

## Importance of Record Keeping

When you went into business, chances are you weren't imagining grand evenings filled with paperwork. Maybe you thought tax records were a thing you would think about once a year and have your accountant deal with. But, the truth is, as you progress in business, you come to realize that record keeping for your taxes needs regular maintenance. In fact, even after you breathe a sigh of relief once that return has been double-checked and sent off to the IRS, you may need to make a change to the document.

That's where the statute of limitations comes in. It refers to the periods of time during which both you and the IRS may make changes to your tax return (not just audits). Those time frames are clearly delineated in IRS publications as follows:

- No limit if you did not file a return

- No limit if you filed a fraudulent return
- Three years after filing if you filed on time (or with extensions), you did not understate your income by 25 percent or greater, and you did not file fraudulently
- Six years after filing if you filed on time (or with extensions) but you understated your income by greater than 25 percent
- If you filed an amended return or already made changes to the original return (like a quick refund claim), either three years after filing or two years after paying the tax
- Seven years from filing for a claim filed for a bad-debt deduction or loss from worthless securities

## *Keeping Appropriate Records*

Aside from letting you know how long you have to make changes to a return, the statute of limitations also lets you know how long the IRS has to audit your return. If an audit occurs, you are going to need all of your tax records to prove your deductions. What does this mean for your record keeping habits? Hang on to those records until any chance of audit has passed.

The following are a few guidelines for making sure you hold

on to the appropriate records long enough:

• Employment Tax Records-If you have employees, you need to save your employment tax records for four years after whichever date comes later, the date payroll taxes were paid or the date they were due. An easy way to do this is simply to keep six separate drawers in your filing cabinet for each tax year. Every year, discard the sixth drawer when it's statute of limitations expires.

• Records for Assets-You have certain assets that are pertinent to your tax return for as long as they remain in the depreciable category. Examples of such assets include your office building, computers, desks, and even your car. If you are depreciating those assets, they will be on your tax return. Otherwise, if you are using Section 179 to expense the assets, you may be able to recapture the depreciable class life.

For example, let's say you purchased a desk for $1,500 and depreciate it over the seven-year Modified Accelerated Cost Recovery System (MACRS) life, which takes eight years. You'll still have to prove depreciation in the eighth year. So, you need the record of the original purchase in the eighth year and through the eleventh year to meet the three-year statute of limitations (the time during which this purchase is subject to auditing). The example works the same if you used Section 179. Any assets with more than a one-year class life should be kept in a separate, permanent file so they don't get tossed out with files whose statutes of limitations have expired.

## *Record Keeping Tips*

As mentioned in the section on employment tax records, you can simplify your file system by devoting separate drawers for each tax year. In those drawers, you'll put any information on assets, income, and other information applicable to your return. The first drawer will be where you put all documents as you acquire them throughout the year. The next drawer is last year's tax documents. The drawer after that contains documents from three years ago, and so on until you reach the year at which your statute of limitations expires.

In order to use this method, it's important that you file your taxes on time or file an extension so you know for sure your specific time frames. At the end of each year, the last drawer gets dumped and you move the other drawers down, starting a new drawer for the current year. It's really simple once you put the system in place. Keep in mind, you can use this system with paperless digital file systems if you like. Record keeping may seem tedious, but remember, it shows you where your business has been and where it's going, like a runner trying to improve their time. You can't improve the numbers if you don't know what they are.

## A Final Word of Caution

If you are already using some of the strategies I have written about in this book, congratulations! You are ahead of most taxpayers, but tax strategy is about optimization. Just about everyday I see examples of poor use of an otherwise great strategy. Don't assume your strategy execution is as good as it can be. I recommend you review every strategy you are using with your tax advisor and ask the following questions:

- Does this strategy work well in my current circumstances?
- Am I using this strategy the best way possible?
- Is there anything I could do to make it better?
- Is my documentation to support this strategy adequate?
- Does this strategy conflict with anything else I am doing?

## *The Importance a Good Accounting System*

A good accounting system won't, in and of itself, make your business more successful. However, if you have a great accounting system and you keep it up to date, your financial life will run much smoother. The reality is you can't optimize your tax strategy without good current financial data. Good accounting is an investment in your future, don't sell yourself short.

Thanks for reading! I wish you well in all your endeavors, especially your quest to avoid overpaying your taxes.